HYPNOTIZE a TiGER

POEMs aBout just aBout EVERYThing

CaLEf BROWN

Christy Ottaviano Books

HENRY HOLT AND COMPANY ◇ NEW YORK

For Greta Cobb, Macy Russell-Brown, and Jennifer Brown

Special thanks to Jennifer Laughran, agent extraordinaire

Henry Holt and Company, LLC. *Publishers since 1866*
175 Fifth Avenue, New York, New York 10010
mackids.com

Library of Congress Cataloging-in-Publication Data
Brown, Calef.
[Poems. Selections]
Hypnotize a tiger : poems about just about everything / Calef Brown ; illustrated
by Calef Brown. — First edition.
pages   cm
Summary: "A whimsical collection of nonsense poetry and art by an
award-winning creator" — Provided by publisher.
ISBN 978-0-8050-9928-7 (hardcover) — ISBN 978-0-8050-9930-0 (ebook)
1. Children's poetry, American.   I. Title.
PS3552.R68525A6 2014   811'.54—dc23   2014041425

Henry Holt books may be purchased for business or promotional use.
For information on bulk purchases, please contact the Macmillan Corporate and Premium Sales
Department at (800) 221-7945 x5442 or by e-mail at specialmarkets@macmillan.com.

First Edition—2015 / Design by Véronique Lefèvre Sweet
Printed in the United States of America by R. R. Donnelley & Sons Company,
Harrisonburg, Virginia

1 3 5 7 9 10 8 6 4 2

THE POEM SCHEME

may contain a gnome theme

The CRITTERVERSE

*Creatures large, small, and off-the-wall—
their tales are often tall.*

SIR PARROT

I handed Sir Parrot
a packet of suet.
He started to chew it
but just couldn't do it.
Instead of the suet,
I gave him some millet.
He shuffled his feet
and proceeded to spill it.
Instead of the millet,
I offered a pellet.
He narrowed his eyes
and would not even smell it.
"This food," said Sir Parrot,
"if that's what you call it,
is very unpleasant,
so open your wallet
and kindly provide me
with ten dollars cash.
I'm off to the village
for bangers and mash."

I only eat cuttlefish from Cuddalore.
Sure, they cost a little more,
but ones from Delhi are sometimes smelly.

I prefer Swiss chard from Mumbai,
which is hard to come by.

CLARENCE

My new puppy, Clarence,
pounced on my allowance.
He shredded half
and ate the balance.
I told my parents
of this occurrence.
"Sorry," they said,
"no allowance insurance."

4

CAMERA BEAR

Very shy, and extremely rare,
the Massachusetts Camera Bear*
stays aware of the local area
through landscape photography.
It shoots the hillsides,
charts the topography,
then posts pictures on a blog—
shots of the cranberry bog,
the best log for back scratching,
and where to find picnickers
(mainly for snack snatching).

*Also known as the Kodakodiak bear.

PIGEON FROGS

Pigeon Frogs!
Pigeon Frogs!
Found on ledges,
hollow logs,
and lily pads
along the gutter.
All day long
they hop and flutter.
Snatching crumbs
and catching flies
with bobbing heads
and bulging eyes.
They peck and pause.
They leap around.
They coo and croak—
a common sound
in city streets
and country bogs.
Pigeon Frogs!
Pigeon Frogs!

Are pigeon frogs pigeon-toed?

Their legs *are* a smidgen bowed.

TADSCHOOL

"Dad," said the tadpole,
"if I went to Toad School
instead of Frog Academy,
would you be mad at me?"
"Fear not, little laddie,"
said Daddy Frog
to the pollywog.
"I'm happy either way.
Work hard, study every day,
and expand your knowledge.
Next stop—
Salamander College!"

THE TOOTHIES

An old log cabin
in a Nordic glen
will, every now and then,
host the Toothies—
a special awards show.
All the beavers in the fjords go.
It features the Golden Choppers Prize
for dental health, incisor size,
and great achievements
in scenery chewing.
The crowd gets tired of viewing
soon after arriving there.
Then they build a dam—
live, on the air.

BO

This is Bo,
the chatty ox.
He talks and talks
and talks and talks.
All about himself, of course.
He seems at risk of going hoarse.
The words come out
with such a force—
at least a mile a minute.
He loves a conversation,
if he alone is in it.

With this beast of burden
you won't get a word in,
even edgewise.
He talks while eating french fries!

GEESE

Who let the geese loose?
They waddled over yonder.
Geese tend to wander,
especially the gander.
He likes to meander to the larder
and devour all the couscous.
Who let the geese loose?

Oh no! Now there are geese loose in the ghee sluice!

Ghee is butter.

Thanks for clarifying.

TURTLE FEZ

"Check out the tassel!"
the Sea Turtle says.
"The one on the top
of my undersea fez!
It follows the currents
and flows with the tide.
It floats in a circle
and snaps to the side.
A tassel will dazzle,"
the Sea Turtle says,
"when pinned to the top
of an undersea fez!"

SEA BATS

Coastal bats
enjoy the view
from high on cliffs
in misty caves.
They like to watch
the frisky waves
when the sea is wild
and misbehaves.

Toad roadkill can be made into stylish open-toad sandals.

THE VULTURE

"Another lunch of dead skunk?
What a stink!
I need to rethink my future,"
thought the vulture.
"I'm uninspired and my soul is sick—
suddenly tired of the same old shtick:
The lonely nights on country roads.
The hasty meals of flattened toads.
This is my diet?
If it died, I try it?
Suppertime is like a riot—
fighting other buzzards
for stinky gizzards
of former lizards and field mice.
A normal dinner would feel *so* nice.
Grilled asparagus and wild rice
without the wretched carrion.
Something vegetarian."

I don't wear sandals—the foot straps and buckles
tickle my toe knuckles and my ankles too.

And this rankles you?

ROOSTER SAYS

"A warm place to roost
and the occasional feast
in a nice restaurant.
What else does a rooster want?
Well, since you asked,
I would love a reprieve
from my least favorite task—
the daily wake-up call.
To wake up and squall
in a barnyard stall
is no fun at all.
Such a caterwaul!
Just once,
I'd like to start the day my way—
with a nice calypso song.
Is that so wrong?"

MY PEEPS

Memorable folks—
these ladies and blokes.
A lively group of unique individuals.
(Sorry, gang, no residuals.)

LAZYHEAD

Take a look at Lazyhead
eating frozen raisin bread,
staring at the television
hanging on the wall.
It's eighty inches tall.
Purchased at the mall.
And all the things that Lazyhead
has never seen and never said
and never thought and never read
will sadly be replaced instead
forever, by the life he led
staring at the television
hanging on the wall.

You've turned into a couch spud.

Ouch, bud!

EZMERALDA

Ezmeralda shaved her head.
Exactly why, she never said.
When, in time,
her hair grew back,
it really came in "handy."
The finger curls, especially,
she thinks are rather dandy.

HUGH

Meet my Belgian friend.
He lives near Bruges, on a farm.
His name is Hugh Jarm.

I once had a dream I was visiting Bruges—
snacking on chocolates while riding a luge.

CAP'N POWER

Mighty Cap'n Power.
He dreamed he was stuck in a flower.
So surreal.
A real ordeal.
It lasted half an hour.
His mood was very sour
when he woke at two o'clock,
tangled in a sleeping bag
and chewing on a sock.

24

I wonder if I have a synapse collapse whenever I begin naps,
and that's why I sleep heavily and soundly
even with revelry around me.

Could be.

TEXARKANA BELLA

Texarkana Bella
in a custom western suit.
So much fun—
she's such a hoot.
She wears one sneaker
and a cowboy boot.

Texarkana Bella
in a fifteen-gallon hat.
So polite—
she's cool like that.
She lives by the river
in a railroad flat.
Where she goes
is "where it's at."
Texarkana Bella.

Sneakers are useless for kicking Hacky Sacks.
Try soccer cleats or hockey socks.

LADY CALDERHAT

Lovely Lady Calderhat.
Everybody calls her that.
She wears a most amazing bonnet—
purple, with a mobile on it.
Upward and downward
it swivels and sways,
exactly in sync
with marimbas she plays.
See her performing
in Washington Square.
Thousands of people
are watching her there.
Completely enchanted,
they stop and they stare
at Lovely Lady Calderhat.
Everybody calls her that.

Lady Calderhat once played bass clarinet in a famous quartet.
The lineup featured Pablo Picasso on keyboards,
Vincent van Gogh on the drums,
and Auguste Renoir on electric guitar
(who, unlike Monet, could actually play).
The band was called Stompe L'oeil, which Duchamp thought coy.

GRETA

Greta can't make up her mind
if she should make up her bed
or practice gymnastics instead.
She likes to jump on the mattress, you see,
which often ends in catastrophe,
with pillows and blankets everywhere,
and then her parents are there
giving her a blank stare.
"Are you aware," they ask,
"that it's one a.m.?"
"Yes," she replies,
"I am."

LOU GNOME

Look who came back home
to Hoboken—
it's Lou Gnome!
Like the G in his name,
Lou is silent.
Completely nonviolent.
He doesn't speak,
even when spoken to.
None of the Gnomes in Hoboken do.

Those that are gnome-schooled
are required to recite the Pledge of the Wee-Gents,
sometimes at huge events.

KNIGHT, SCHOOLED

"Heed my words, Young Lad,"
said the Brave Knight.
"Never tease or antagonize
harmless dragonflies."
"Or dragons, either,"
said the Young Lad.
"It isn't right."
"Touché," said the Brave Knight.

THE INSECT SECTION

*A concise selection of rhyming folly,
both creepy and crawly.*

PUPAE

Just because we're pupae,
people give us the poop-eye.
They unfairly dismiss every chrysalis,
but only rarely do they consider this:

Soon we'll all be butterflies,
flitting through the flowers.
Highly prized in all your eyes.
Up with pupa powers!

LIKE A LOUSE

I would hate to be a louse—
always feeling lousy,
even when overjoyed
or pleasantly drowsy.
If, for example,
I won a prize
or bought a new house,
"I'm thrilled," I would say,
"but I feel like a louse."

I applied for a lice license twice.
They said I lied, which wasn't nice.

ANTS

I don't mean to nitpick,
but I went to a picnic,
and ants were rampant!
I saw one take a crumpet,
but I didn't stamp it.
That's not my style.
With a friendly smile,
I separated ant from crumpet.
"If you don't like it," I whispered,
"you can lump it."

According to those who study entomology, an ant apology is rare.

FLEAS

Fleas irk us.
Except, of course,
in a flea circus.
Then they charm us.
All is forgiven.
How can they harm us
on a highwire
or a flying trapeze?
Quite a flip-flop—
applauding for fleas.

MY HIVE

Early this morning
without any warning,
and much to my chagrin,
I awoke with a beehive
on the underside of my chin.
What a way for the day to begin!
Now I can't nod
or play the violin.
The pollen on my collar
is drying out my skin.
And the din!
Buzzing and droning,
every waking hour.
They won't let me eat
or take a shower.
On the brighter side,
the bees all decided
that I would be included
when they sell the honey.
I *could* use the money.

I wonder: Do baby birds make good beekeepers,
since they're beak eepers?

EEP EEP EEP EEP

Centipede on my rented tweed!

INFESTED

"Ants in my pants!" cried Lance.
"Fleas in my chemise!" screamed Louise.
"Hornet in my hairnet!" blared Yvette.
"Insect free!" yelled Ricky Lee.
"Lucky me!"
"Wait and see,
They'll get their chance!"
shouted Yvette, Louise, and Lance.

I once saw a gorilla feed a millipede a vanilla seed.

A silly deed.

Agreed.

INTERVIEW WITH A TERMITE

Good afternoon.

Cheers.

Mr. Termite, sir,
what makes you a picky eater?
Why don't you like cedar?

*I'm very choosy
about the wood I chew.
Wouldn't you be too?*

I would, indeed.
Let's proceed.
For daily sustenance,
what do you need?

*Imported toothpicks
of the finest oak
dipped in honey
and left to soak
in several small batches.*

How about kitchen matches?

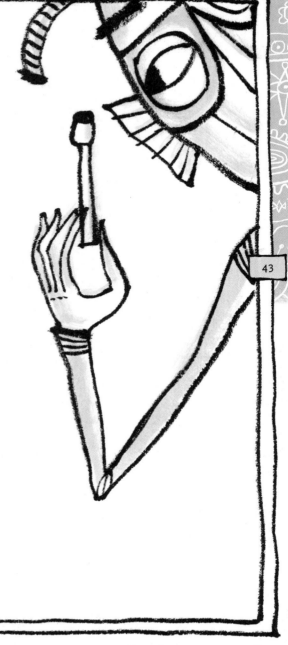

Those are mostly Scots pine
with lots of knots
so I often decline.
Not much else to say.
Their flavor is just okay,
nothing too incredible.
They're even less edible
with sulfur on the tips,
which causes ulcers
and chapped lips.
The phosphorus and ether
aren't too good for us either.

What was your finest meal?

My family and I
were lucky enough to share
a most delicious pair
of tongue depressors
owned by our hosts . . .

two young professors
at a nearby med school.
Thinking about it now
makes my head drool—
meaning, I sweat.
When recalling great meals
that's how I get.

What about sawdust,
do you eschew it?

No, not at all.
It must, however, be rolled in a ball
with a splinter for a garnish.

Free, I would guess, of any varnish.

That's correct.
And no shellac or deck stain.
No one likes gas and back pain!

Quite true.

And now, I'm afraid,
it's time to say adieu.

Good day to you too.

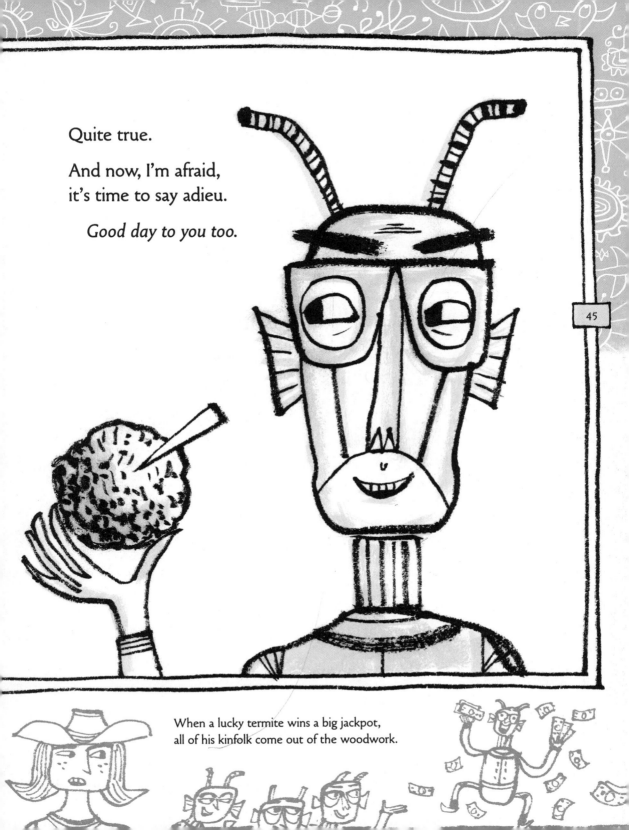

When a lucky termite wins a big jackpot,
all of his kinfolk come out of the woodwork.

POEMS
of a
PARTICULAR
VEHICULAR
NATURE

Roll, hover, fly
over road, sea, sky!

VELOCIPEDE

Great-great-grandpa
guides his steed
on winding roads
at awesome speed.
He rides a great velocipede.
Front wheel giant.
Back wheel tiny.
Swift and silent.
Tall and shiny.

Remember: If your velocipede proceeds less speedily,
recede to the median immediately!

MY SKATEBOARD

I never get bored
on my skateboard.
So many things to skate toward:
The home of a good chum.
The sound of a bass drum.
And things to skate away from:
An old newsstand.
A lame blues band.
Few grown-ups understand
the thrill of a skateboard
and the great reward
of smooth, limitless travel.
My nemesis is gravel.

Why is it called a boarding school, if there's a no-skateboarding rule?
Not cool!

UFOS

If you have foes
in UFOs,
you'd better watch the skies.
Angry martians popping by—
not a nice surprise.

If you have *pals*
from outer space,
that could be a plus.
Instant rides to anywhere
surely beat the bus.

A NICE ROAD TRUCKER

I'm a Nice Road Trucker.
My handle is Wayne.
My favorite route to travel
is a country lane.
Turnpikes and traffic
are bad for the brain.
Me and a freeway?
Never the twain.

Scenery is key for me—
it keeps me sane.
Driving over mountains
in a misty rain.
Find me out in Cali
or the coast of Maine.
I'm a Nice Road Trucker.
My handle is Wayne.

MIKE'S TRIKE

When Mike was just a tyke,
he built himself a trike.
Oversized and motorized
for speeding down the pike.
Policemen never bothered Mike
for driving super fast.
"We'd likely do the same," they'd say.
"It looks like such a blast!"

CARSICK

Car rides have always
been awful for me.
I try not to look,
but as soon as I see
that the needle is pointing
to forty-three
on the ol' speedometer,
I'm a vomiter.

SKYSCRAPER ROCKET

Skyscraper Rocket
has hundreds of floors.
The windows are closing
and so are the doors.
Into the heavens
it suddenly roars.
Residents cheer
as the edifice soars.
"Comets!" they holler.
"A planet!
A quasar!
Look at that star cloud!
How brilliant the rays are!"

HOVERBUS!

I had a dream
that my bus stop
was on an ice floe.
A crazy notion.
Mighty nice, though,
because the school bus
was a hovercraft!
(However daft that might seem.)
And soon I was driving.
A sweet dream!

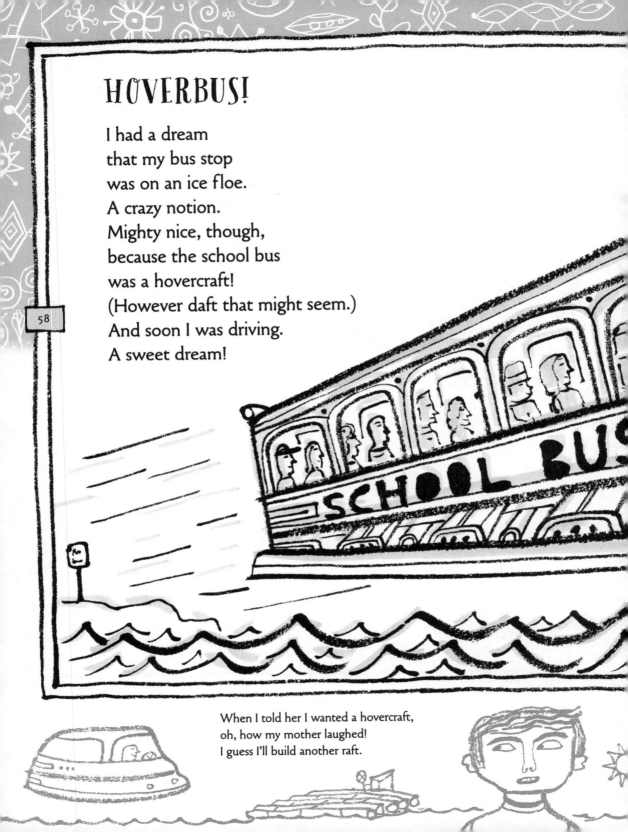

When I told her I wanted a hovercraft,
oh, how my mother laughed!
I guess I'll build another raft.

SCHOOLISHNESS

*T*here will not be a quiz or a test.*

*Except by specific request.

62

HALLWAYS

I'm so confused.
In a daze, always.
Constantly fooled
by school hallways.
I call it the "hall maze."

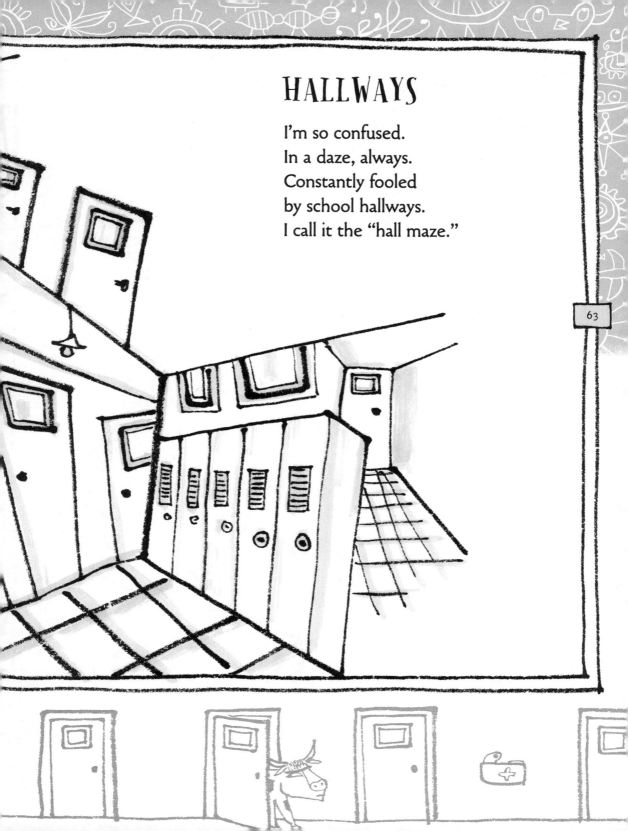

PERCIVAL

There once was a lad
named Percival,
who was quite convinced
he was invincible.
Not too sensible.
He stuck out his tongue
at the school principal,
who, luckily for Percival,
was merciful.

64

TOMATO DEMAND

The teachers
and students
in every grade
were very afraid
of chef Alfredo's
stuffed tomatoes,
but everyone ate 'em.
He made a tomato ultimatum.

Forcing compliance through orders and decrees?
Oh, *please!*

HEAVY LOAD

I think I need a forklift
to lift my backpack.
So many textbooks
in my knapsack,
I fear a back-snap.
Perhaps I'll try a pack mule.
"Giddyup!
Back to school!"

With my rep as a schlepper I could usurp a Sherpa!

FOODIE BULLY

Today's special
cooked up by Sully,
the culinary school bully,
is a knuckle panino
and a cup of clobber broth
topped with slobber froth.
No substitutions.

Don't worry—Sully will get his just deserts.

Justice hurts!

THE GYM TEACHERS

They do not, ordinarily,
have pointy teeth of enormous size
and scary greenish eyes,
so my classmates and I
were rather surprised
by the ghoulish faces and glum features.
Something is wrong with the gym teachers!
They crouch in the bleachers
like sneaker-clad sand fleas.
Their whistles are deafening—
louder than banshees
on a noise spree.
Here's what annoys me:
They make us do battle
in long games of "dodgebull."
(With actual cattle—a giant garage-full!)
Do we look like matadors?!
To them, it doesn't matter, of course,
having been possessed, I would guess,
by some sort of beast-nest,
or a throng of Brothers Grimm creatures.
Something is wrong with the gym teachers!

THE COUGH

On Monday I awoke
with one wee cough.
"I think I'll take the week off,"
I said to my dad,
playing it cool.
He, being a man of few words,
pointed toward my school.

SNOW DAY

I'm always prepared
when a snow day's declared,
so why do I fret so?
I get so nutso
in my noggin.
Right from the get-go
I grab a toboggan.
The first few flakes
are all it takes—
I'm on a sled
with no brakes.
I ski, snowboard,
then build a snow fort.
I just *go for it*
from sunup to sundown.
That's the rundown.

FACTS POETIC

*Not exactly provable
but groovy nonetheless.
It's fun to guess:
Are they extremely silly?
Totally true?
Possibly both?
It's up to you!*

BIG-HAIR CATS

When cougars and lynxes
get fur stuck in their larynxes,
they cough up hairballs
like an ordinary kitty.
It isn't very pretty,
not in the least,
to see a gob of gooey fleece
released by such a noble beast.

What would you do if you were bitten
but also smitten by the same stray kitten?

Forgive, forget, and adopt a new pet!

ONIONS

A fresh, juicy onion
makes a fine companion
at a class reunion.
Need you ask why?
To make your former bully cry!

THISTLE GUARDS

Many thistle growers
hire whistle blowers
to keep weasels and possums
from stealing thistle blossoms.

JURASSIC BBQ

Giant prehistoric critters
once used volcanic craters
to cook gigantic fritters
and titanic taters.
This was disrupted
by massive eruptions,
resulting in fossilized critter matter
embedded in petrified fritter batter.

I dreamed that my living room carpet
was a bubbling tar pit
and I was a hapless mastodon.

                        How fast were you gone?

I didn't last until dawn.

ROMAN PETS

As scholars have shown,
and is now widely known,
everyone in ancient Rome
kept a pet at home.
They even found a dog brush
in a catacomb.

A puppy at play
on the Appian Way
was happy to say
he was not in Pompeii.

GOPHERS

It's rather surprising
that gophers,
not groundhogs,
are the ones who act like pigs
whenever they pilfer figs.
Go figure.

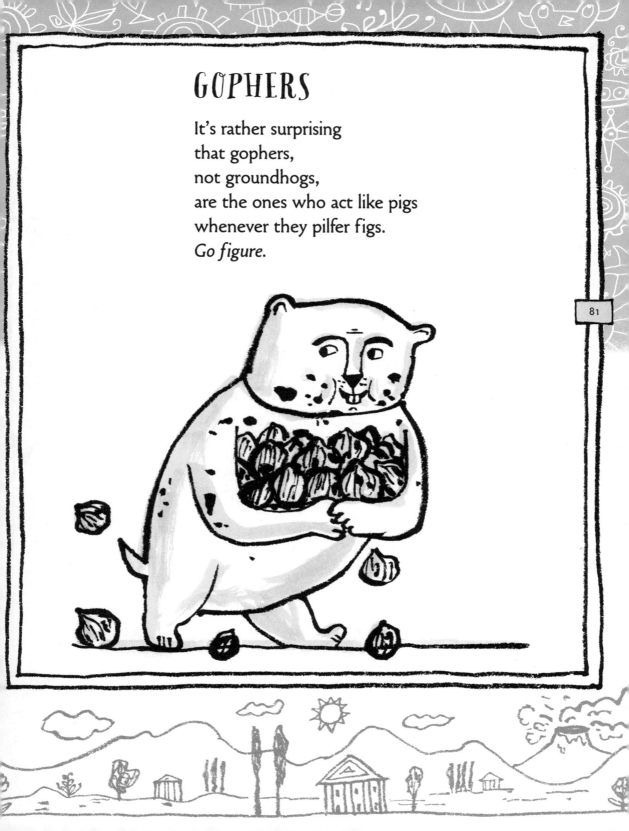

ICARUS DELIVERED

Before there was Christmas
and Old St. Nicholas,
the legendary Icarus
flew from the Acropolis
to every town and metropolis,
delivering pickled licorice
to the fickle populace.

He was not, by the way,
outdone by the hot sun
or the humid weather.
Icarus was ticklish—
his toe touched a feather.
It's risky to giggle
while trying to fly.
You chuckle and wriggle,
and then it's . . .
good-bye.

TUBADOURS

Tuba-playing troubadours
have tuba doors and tuba stiles
installed in all their domiciles
for easy entry and exit.
With a normal door
the tuba wrecks it.

Marching bands are disbanding everywhere,
except in Manitoba, where they can still man a tuba.

DANGERUFF

If left untreated,
ordinary dandruff
can turn to dangeruff,
which is very hazardous
and sometimes even blizzardous.
Clouds of flakes
and snow-white boulders
swirl on necks
and drift on shoulders.

SLED DOGS

All of the dogs
on dogsled teams
are fully expected
to stay connected
even when it isn't winter yet.
Not with harnesses,
they phone and use the Internet.

And now, excerpts from dogs' letters
to dogsledders.

"Dude, stop yelling 'Mush!' so much.
Enough with the whips and such!"

PANDORADOX

There are scores of peacocks
and adorable pandas
in Pandora's box
that nobody talks about.
These, along with the daffodils
and golden hollyhocks,
are, indeed, a paradox.

"We could have won the Iditarod!"   "You're such a quitter, Todd!"

FROZEN OBOE

An ordinary oboe, if played in an igloo,
sounds just like a refrigerated didgeridoo.

MINOTAURS

Minotaurs, as a matter of course,
are not afraid of matadors,
whom they consider a nuisance,
like saddle sores.

WORD CRASHES

*Also known as portmanteaus.
Ever heard of those?
A bit weird, I suppose—
words that combine and intertwine,
but this is where they shine!*

MR. NEWBERG

92

Mister Roger Newberg
sports an **ELEGANTOUPEE**.

FLAMINGOPHERS!

THIRTEENEWTS reside inside it,
much to his dismay.

KANGAROOSTERRAPINS!

TV MINDY

Mindy's **FAVORITELEVISION**
sits upon a ladder.

She watches the **SILLIESTUPIDESTUFF**—
it doesn't seem to matter.

EDUCATEDONUT

ARISTOCRATICANOE

LI'L GORILLA

This **GROUCHYOUNGORILLA** hasn't gotten very far.

Some thoughtless bug has just unplugged his **NICELECTRICAR**.

AGITATEDANDELION

CONDESCENDINGLUE

CROC AND ALLI

An **ALLIGATORABBIT** pops his head out of a hat.

The clever **MAGICROCODILE** knows lots of tricks like that.

INCOHERENTELEVISION

OVEREAGEROCK

THE STORK

These **RARENCHANTINGARDENS**
are a lovely place to rest.

ONENORMOUSTORK
decides to stop and build a nest.

OSTENTATIOUSALAMANDER

ENERGETICLOCK

UNDERWATERUTABAGA

FLYINGHOULISHAT

OGRE AND FRIENDS

There's an **OGREATINGUMDROPS**
on an ivy-covered wall.

EAGEROUNDISHAMSTERS
are hoping some will fall.

WINDOWASHINGARGOYLE

SUPERSONICAT

HIPPOS

A pair of **SLUGGISHIPPOS** amble slowly down the lane.

They plan to take a trip aboard the next **CONVENIENTRAIN**.

AUTOMATICOATTAILIFTER

LARGECCENTRICOMB

YAK AND WOODY

Observe the **MELLOWOODCHUCK** and the **NERVOUSMELLYAK**.

Guess which one
will soon become
a **TYRANNOSAURUSNACK**.

DECORATEDACHSHUNDOG

HORRIDANCINGNOME

SPECIAL DELIVERY

SEVERALARGERANIUMS arrive from Kathmandu,

delivered by a bellhop to a **BEATNIKANGAROO**.

The FAMOUSMILINGURU
answers all your questions why.

SHOPPER CHERUBIC

A **CHERUBUYINGROCERIES**
wants to bake a tasty pie.

TENDERIPERSIMMONS
seem to be in good supply.

Then nods his head politely—
his way of SAYINGOOD-BYE.

GOOD
(and not so good)
EATS

*E*dible rarities,
culinary peculiarities,
and all things epicurean!
(Except for durians. They stink!)

My tomcat Caesar is a doozer of a mouser.
He's a mouse dowser!

CATSUP CATS

The cats upon the mountaintop
make catsup for the town.
This involves tomatoes
and stomping up and down.
The catsup in the wooden vats
is funneled into jars.
The jars go into boxes,
and the boxes into cars.
The cats upon the mountaintop
descend upon the town,
and cats upon the village green
buy catsup by the pound.

I once had a blouse made of cheesecloth,
but a mouse chewed the sleeves off.

NOT BERRY

I don't like to use the word *berry*.
I tend to call blueberries *blues*.
Huckles and *strawbs*
I gobble in gobs.
For stuffing it's *crans* that I use.
I'm wary of *boysens*
and don't care for *muls*,
but *logans* I never refuse.
I don't like to use the word *berry*—
a habit I hope you'll excuse.

Speaking of excuses, you forgot to mention *gooses*
(not the ones that are loose; those that make juice).

THE LOOFAH TORTE

First created
in a Nevada kitchenette
(possibly to win a bet)
the little-known Loofah Torte
is similar to sponge cake,
but more of a plunge to take
in terms of taste.
After your first bite,
you *will* make a face—
most likely an ugly scowl.
It's like a soggy towel, half wrung,
that gently scrubs your tongue
while you chew and chew and chew.
You think you'll never smile again,
but suddenly you do!
Your tongue is bright,
completely clean!
Try one tonight
and see what I mean!

MY FALAFEL

While riding my bicycle,
eating falafel,
I somehow fell off on my head.
It really felt awful—
"I lost my falafel!"
That was the first thing I said.
My mother was tearful.
She gave me an earful
and offered a waffle instead.
I still love falafel
but now I'm more careful—
I eat it at home in my bed.

Eating on the run may seem like fun,
but it's actually *muy peligroso*.
I don't think so, I know so!

MANGO MAIL

A mango fresh from Bangladesh
appeared upon my welcome mat.
I must admit I welcome that—
when snacks arrive from distant lands,
it's such a joy I clap my hands
and rush outside to pick a pear.
I choose a place and send it there,
so someone else I'll never meet
can be surprised and have a treat.

ROYAL GRAVY

When storms arise
and things get wavy
aboard the Royal Navy Boats,
the cooks remove the gravy
from the Royal Gravy Boats
and store it in a soup tureen
equipped with a lid.
Then they add scallops
wrapped in squid—
a favorite recipe
of Captain Kidd.

On a related note—
delicious nectar from nectarines
will turn to goop in soup tureens
if scooped sloppily. Do it properly!

BUBBLE CRUMBS

When a soap bubble
goes POP,
the tiny bits that drop
are known as bubble crumbs.
The trouble comes
when they land in a coffee cup
or end up on a piece of cantaloupe.
Do you detect
a hint of soap
in chicken soup
or pickled plums?
The likely culprit
(you guessed it)
is bubble crumbs.

This mulligatawny stew
has a subtle whiff of shampoo.

FROMAGE FROM RAJ ☆

OPEN

BISCOTTI CHOP

I own my own biscotti shop
and this is what I do:
I practice my karate chop
and snap a few in two.

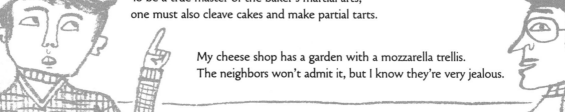

To be a true master of the baker's martial arts,
one must also cleave cakes and make partial tarts.

My cheese shop has a garden with a mozzarella trellis.
The neighbors won't admit it, but I know they're very jealous.

THE SNACK PLAN

This is the plan:
From dawn till dusk
on the Fourth of July,
my best pals and I
will gorge on snacks
while we lie on our backs
in hammocks like lummoxes.
"Please don't!" my stomach says.

Some tummies are such fuddy-duddies!
Should he listen to his gut, or pig out with his buddies?

LICORICE FISH

I'm a very cautious guy.
I generally keep a close eye
on all my favorite chow,
but someone, somehow,
has been adding licorice
to my dishes of tuna fish.
I have absolutely no clue
as to who is doing this
but must admit I'm curious.
If it wasn't so delicious,
I'd be furious!

117

Remember: He who gorges, tortures the belly.

Plus, things can get, well, smelly.

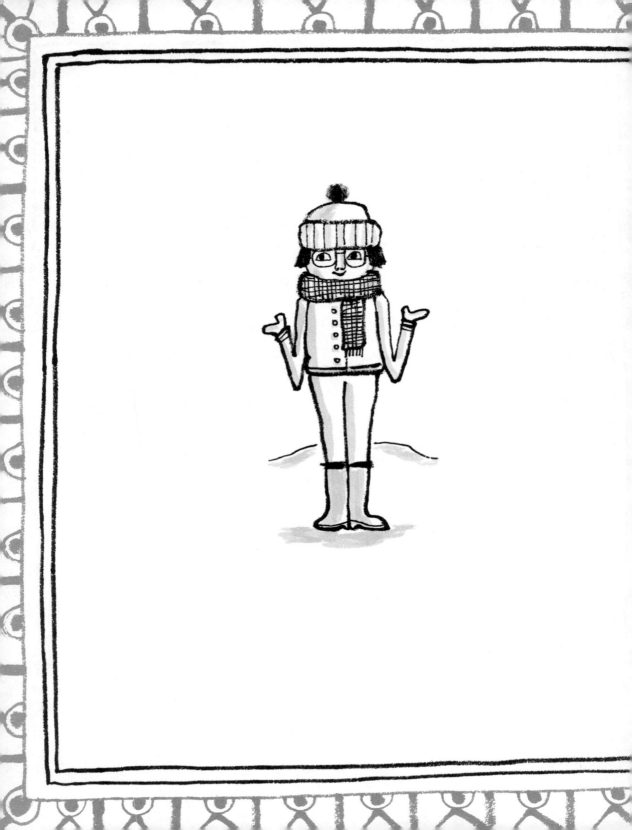

MiSCELLANEOUS SiLLINESS

*They will hopefully
strike a chord—
the assorted themes explored
in this poem smorgasbord.*

THE DOUBLENOSE HOTEL

Are you a savvy traveler
with a keen sense of smell?
If so, the only place to go
is The Doublenose Hotel.
From the grand ballroom
to the penthouse café,
it's a nasal buffet—
a complex bouquet
of rare perfumes.
Free aroma service
in all the rooms.
You can order an odor
at any odd hour.
The essence of mint
or an exotic flower.
The water in the shower
is sweetly scented,
and every suite is vented
in case it gets too "fragrancy."
Arrive early—there's rarely a vacancy
at the famous inn that smells so swell—
The Doublenose Hotel.

A bit of trivia:
This olfactory lodge was once a large old factory.

THE UPSIDE

I'm totally lost,
but at least I'm not frostbit.
I can't find the ridge
or the bridge where I crossed it.
Supplies are so low.
Should I go?
Should I risk it?
I still have some grease
on a piece of a biscuit.
Tucked in my cap
was a map, but I tossed it.
I'm totally lost,
but at least I'm not frostbit.

SATELLITES

Satellites know of our whereabouts.
Within a few inches or thereabouts.
Is this something anyone cares about?
They'll tell us, I hope, when there's bears about.

A satellite, when it plummets like an asteroid, is best to avoid.

WHO?

Who can trap a ninja
with a ginger snap?
Or hypnotize a tiger
with a finger tap?
Who can stop a chopper
with a paper clip?
Or excavate a crater
with a carrot chip?
Who can catch a comet
with a simple paper sack?
Or perforate a freighter
with an ordinary tack?
Who can grow a garden
with a single drop of dew?
How about a clue?
Is it me, or is it you?

MY NEST EGG

This is so exciting!
I can't believe I'm here.
It's time to take the money
I've been saving every year
and make a good investment
so I'll never have to fear.
This will be my nest egg
when I finish my career.
My hand is up.
My bid is in.
I hear the auctioneer—
"Seven thousand dollars
for the candy chandelier!"

I'm not sure how aware you are
of how dumb you look playing air guitar,
but something must be said.
Please adjust your head.

JUST AS WELL

I can play the banjo,
but not with my elbow.
I guess it's just as well, though.
If I could somehow do so,
my fingers might get jealous,
and they're such nice fellas.

I can play "Little Old Cupola from Tupelo"!

Not as well as Mott the Hoople, though.

GO, MUSIC!

Sing a song of supermarkets.
Bellow out a tune.
Compose a lonely ballad
of a monkey on the moon.
Write an operetta
for a friend you've never met.
Play a blue sonata
on a purple clarinet.
Score a future feature film.
Study tambourine.
Reinvent the sousaphone
and burst upon the scene.
Learn to yodel Paganini.
Teach yourself to croon.
Hold a note
from Friday night
till Tuesday afternoon.

129

Q & A

with
Calef BROWN

Q & A WITH CALEF BROWN

Tell us about your early days.

*My life began in a tree fort
in Shreveport, Louisiana.
A sort of breezy cabana
with one of those fantastic lawns—
the kind with gnomes and plastic swans.
I was a weaselly child,
easily riled and wildly erratic,
full of dramatic "tin-drum tantrums"—
the loudest kind.
My parents, who didn't seem to mind,
were more inclined
to write poems and be quiet,
so I decided to try it.
This stood me in good stead
during the years ahead
when my least-worst ability
turned out to be verse facility.*

What did you do before becoming a poet and artist?

My first job involved housebreaking elephants,
which required both keen intelligence and doo-doo diligence.
Then I delivered limes to Leominster and news to Coalcastle
but was less than enthused with the whole hassle.
I still have a part-time gig driving the Beatle Shuttle.
My route is Liverpool to Kidneypuddle.

Do you like to travel?

It sounds, I know, totally insane,
but I will hop, skip, and jump on a plane
with a minimum of cajoling.
I'm off to Minsk for some bowling!

Favorite and least favorite foods?

I love breakfast soups,
and I just became aware of a stew
made with tiramisu and asparagus too . . .

I'm disgusted by custard.
I've never discussed it.
And pudding is sneaky.
I don't really trust it.

Were you ever a sensible person?

No, I've always been impractical—practically incorrigible.
I just bought a dirigible, which is huge and unstorageable.

What are your preferred fashion choices?

I stole my style from mountain goats—
wooly scarves and overcoats.
But I don't often wear a caftan or a shawl.
Very seldom, if at all.
Same goes for a cape or a cloak.
Just a regular bloke, not too macho.
Not much of a honcho.
I will, in a pinch, wear a poncho
with a couple of bandoleros.
I load 'em with breadsticks to feed the sparrows.

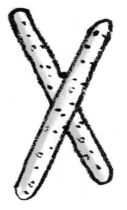

Are you a creature of habit?

I have a strict daily routine.
Every morning at six fifteen:
I walk in Morocco,
I stroll in Kowloon.
I jog in Chicago,
I run in Rangoon.
I dance in Gdansk,
and I swim in Cologne.
I breathe the sea air
in Sierra Leone.
Then I go home
and write a poem.

Do you have a hobby?

Reverse-gardening.
I plant beets and carrots backward,
pointing upward,
to make it fun for the rabbits.
It's one of my wonderful habits.

Any other artists in the family?

> My grandma, who lives in New Jersey,
> sells ceramics there.
> She's famous for her garden gnomes
> and huge "Paramus hair."

How would you describe yourself?

> A misfit sophisticate.
> I can't get the gist of it.
> It's easier to be an aristocrat.
> Anyone can master that.
> All it requires
> is a hat and a monocle.
> Along with a fondness
> for words like ironical.

What's your favorite color?

> My favorite color is blue.
> It's never a dolorous hue.

What does your future hold?

If I may be so bold,
allow me to lay out my retirement plan:
It involves a big lottery check
and a catamaran.
I will sail to a sunny port
in South Amiracle.
I will build a home there.
Possibly spherical.
My days will be full
as I slowly grow older
writing and sketching
while perched on a boulder
at the edge of town.
Hunkering down,
far from the crazy bazaars
and the noise of the cars,
I will scribble out my
memoirs—
all my remembrances.
Written in verse.
Fragments of sentences.

Any parting thoughts?

Thank you all for reading.
I hope you enjoyed my book—
the artwork and wordplay.
Creating it was a whirlwind!
(In a good way.)
Not to be a pest,
but I'd like to suggest
that every now and then,
whenever you have a yen,
pick up a pencil, a pen,
a tablet, or a laptop,
at home or at a bus stop,
and write your own poems
about just about anything,
or everything,
or nothing at all.
Heed the call!

Fondly,

Calef Brown

P.S. And remember: Words are like friends. It helps to know lots—
for sentences, paragraphs, stories, and thoughts.
(Not to mention sonnets, speeches, and choruses.)
Hooray for dictionaries and thesauruses!